SELECTION PERFECTION

A Rock-Solid Premarital Guide For You

Hasan Clay, B.S., MBA
&
Naa'ila Clay, B.A., MS

Copyright © 2021 Hasan and Naa'ila Clay.

All rights reserved. No portion of this book may be reproduced mechanically, electronically, or by any other means, including photocopying, without the written permission of the publisher. It is illegal to copy this book, post it on a website, or distribute it by any other means without permission from the publisher.

Table of Contents

Introduction 1

Chapter One: Have A Genius Relationship 4

Chapter Two: The Flaws Of Attraction 25

Chapter Three: Fear Factor 38

Chapter Four: Get Your "Ish" Together 42

Chapter Five: Issa No For Me 54

Chapter Six: *"What Do You Bring To The Table?"* 64

Chapter Seven: Undoing Being Unmarried 73

Chapter Eight: "Trick Or Treat" 76

References 88

Introduction

When folks begin to speak about relationships, dating, and marriage, fear engulfs their head and heart. It's even truer when one lives in a society perpetuating values, principles, and sexuality about love that doesn't equal to what their love life looks like on a Saturday evening. After some time, you question the validity of the heart suggestions around you. Soon, you begin to ask yourself, particularly if you've been unmarried for several years or continue to marry wrongly.

During these weird and unstable times, many seek freedom from doubt through experts, healers, elders, and sometimes, folks listen to the misguidance of their pain. Whatever you believe will work at the time! Before marriage, we did our groundwork to improve relationships. Our mistake was a common one. Our view was more intently focused on others versus self. After some time, we got tired of our mess and took matters into our hands. Who better to handle you than you?

LOL! Whoa! Were we in for a double whammy! We learned we didn't like some of the things uncovered about ourselves. If it was difficult for us to have and to hold, who'd wanna do this with us forever? Until you devise a plan to smell your funk, you haven't developed a strategy! This process takes time, and you get the benefit of it.

We're stepping to the idea of mastering the ability to select your PERSON in a way cynics and folks suffering from loneliness will warn you against doing. Mentally, kick all of the ideas and expectations you've heard about "getting to know someone" to the curb. Be a part of the sanctity of self-exploration and the temporary throbbing pain of learning something new.

Jonathon Ive, a designer of Apple Inc. tech products, said, "It's very easy to be different, but very difficult to be better." What if you seize this moment to be better and not stumble at the idea of difficulty?

You've done it before. Sometimes, it worked out, and other times, not. Have you ever felt life was like a treadmill with you doing the same mental and emotional workout each day? Who hasn't?!

During the process, the voice in your head repeats the mantra of the naysayers, which blocks you from manifesting the intimate connection you desire. This is where you can transform, not by force but by choice. This is not a last-ditch effort to get married. This is one of your first repositionings! You have finally chosen to trust your intuitive knowing, get inspired by experts, and change the patterns of what has gone off the relationship road previously.

Remember when you wanted to be in control, and you believed you were. You told folks precisely what you wanted from a man or a woman. Your "Act Right" list was well-rehearsed, and you could recite it on demand. You knew what you would do when someone said this, and you had a response in your pocket if someone said that. What you did not know is that with this desire to control and drive the direction of the relationship, especially in the early stages, you unintentionally urged folks to burn up the road and leave you alone.

Being vulnerable, which includes trusting yourself before anyone else, is one of the most viable tools you need in this process. What have you done to prepare yourself to be vulnerable? Hmmm…..This process ain't about what you are gonna do to prep yourself for game, delete narcissists from your life, or any other popular marriage or relationship buzz words. You're going to get to pay attention to you and how you show up with your attachment patterns, love history, and "Ain't Nobody Got Time Fuh That" expectations in your head.

CHAPTER ONE
~
HAVE A GENIUS RELATIONSHIP

The way folks find love follows technological trends. Really quickly…think of the different ways your friends or family members have met Bae. It's mind-boggling all of the corners, clicks, and virtual rooms used for sweet talk. For what reason should the start of your love story be any different? It shouldn't! Don't limit yourself either. Meet them in any location, allowing you to be safe, to know this person has good hygiene and offers comfort for the in-depth conversations ya'll need to learn about one another. In-person. Facetime. On social media. Snail Mail. Your inbox. Your email. Via text. It can be a lot of fun.

Speaking of text, how many times have you received the random but so personalized "You-Are-Important-And-Everything" text in the morning? There's one issue; your bills, lifestyle, goals, vision board, and mental space won't allow for "WYD Beautiful?" texts. What do you do when you like this person, but this is how this person does dating and courtship, and you're uninterested in this method?

Do you look at your phone, frown, and hit "Block This Caller"? You don't do group texts sent by a playa or a thirsty chic with good teeth. Not your type at all!

Or do you take the time to say, "It felt good to hear from you. Thank you. My mornings are rushed and flustered as it is. I almost didn't see your text. Maybe we can connect via text in a more personable way later in the day?"

What choice do you make? What have you done in the past when a person didn't measure up to the "Bae" persona created in your head? It can be grueling to decide what to do in this uncertain territory.

Many have mentally identified a specific person for the potential role of "Forever Love of My Life." You've imagined your families meeting one another. In your head, you're doing a happy dance about what is to be manifested in your love life. Each day, you want to know more and more about this person. The genuine conversation flows like love in motion. You've imagined it all many times over! This bond feels like kindred-spirit conversations. You've never talked back and forth like this for hours with another person.

In your head, this is the ultimate relationship for you. You know it is possible to encounter this person, on earth, at any time. And yet, when you believe you may have, you get a "You-Are-Important-And-Everything" text in the morning. SMH…not what you planned at all.

What do you do when you like this person, but not this part of them? How do you decide which parts to negotiate and what areas to set a limit on because of who you naturally are as a person? What if this incident or interaction with this person means nothing or is indicative of choices and a lifestyle you know nothing about as of yet?

Let's say you have another set of issues, such as someone fading to black on you. Picture this. You talk almost nonstop for days straight. You talk first thing in the morning and then make the last human connection of the day at night. Life gets busy, and you miss a day or two. S'ok. You're on the go, people. This was bound to happen.

Then, the chatting never picks up the same pace. You're fine. Truthfully, it was extra and all about the warm fuzzies for you anyway. Neither of you could continue that high level of interaction indefinitely anyway. However, this person says you're playing games with their heart, insincere and fake. You can hardly respond and feel flabbergasted anyone would say such a thing. For the other party, you don't do enough to keep their interest. You may be 'the other party,' and to someone else, you seem thirsty or extra. Who's right when someone's heart is on the line?

For example, sending a friendly text is a nice gesture. Wanting a response within minutes and forwarding another text when it doesn't happen is questionable. This, after bombarding someone with texts, following up by investigating their social media activity is too much. See how quickly it can escalate. There's a level to this! Dialogue and desperation are not the same! Getting caught in the façade of regular attention, lots of communication, and sweet words will lead to a piss-poor partner every time. Trust and believe, someone blowing up your phone and talking you to sleep at night, knowing each of you have to go to work in the morning, is not a sign of an emotional connection. It could be some closet symptoms of a personality disorder or control issues, but you decide to label it affection and run with it.

You recall the standards you had when no one was calling you.

Folks act all hard and have committed boundaries until they like someone! Loosening the standards and boundaries you held when your phone wasn't ringing is unfair to you and leaves you exposed to a person unable to love you with good intent. Don't deny the risky consequences of taking shortcuts because someone is cute or has the seal of approval of your family. Take a holistic approach to how others experience you and how you want a person to feel and think in a marriage with you.

All Relationships Matter. Even the ones you ended.

What you do with this data dramatically determines how you proceed when connecting with others, including your Future Bae. Recognizing the high-tech insider information about yourself when you see it will be your gift to yourself. Using it for your benefit will be a skill to master. Allowing someone to match and echo your innate love skills creates the marriage of a lifetime.

Having all this talk with someone means nothing if you don't use it to learn more about yourself. Repeating the list of your preferences in an ideal partner won't always be what you need in a partner. Way too often, we ask for traits and personalities to keep us stagnant, to create an unrealistic lifestyle, and to get mad when it doesn't happen. Talking with someone for hours over coffee or binge-watching your favorite Netflix series over the phone doesn't tell much about who a person is on an hour-by-hour and day-to-day basis. Most people can act right until coffee gets cold or through a movie and discussion. Since this isn't about pretending, but being legit and authentic, let's put it on paper. There's much power in writing down a commitment and affirmation to yourself.

How do you want your spouse to experience you, and what will you do to make it happen? Please, steer away from the fluff. Giving a long list of action words you'd see on a dating site isn't ingenuity. For example, stating, "My Bae will find me to be honest." This sounds good. No one wants a lifelong commitment with a liar. That means more is how honesty looks coming from you.

To one person, honesty may look like being open about larger issues, but for fibs, it's ok to flub the truth a bit. For someone out there, this would piss them off. And for that reason, it's integral to know what words to mean another person. You hear something, and as many folks do, you translate it through the filter of your life. Find out the meaning the person intended to convey before assuming you know. Quit hearing something that feels good and saying, "I Do!" No, you do not! Not anymore!

Now, to your list! Oh, and get a notebook! You'll need paper for this enlightenment! It'll be fun to record this journey.

How do you want your spouse to experience you? Spiritually. Sexually. As a friend. With daily household functions. As a parent to a stepchild or future children.

- _____

- _____

- _____

- _____

- _____

What will you do to create these experiences? Answer this question for each category/section listed above.

1. _____

2. _____

3. _____

4. _____

5. _____

How will your marriage reflect your success with achieving these goals? What will be happening between you & your spouse? What will your interactions look like?

1. _____

2. _____

3. _____

4. _____

5. _____

Other questions and topics to ponder:

Are you marrying someone who wants to have the experiences you're offering?

If your Future Bae doesn't respond to the experience you seek to create the way you'd prefer, can you still consider it a success?

The experiences you desire to create are your natural methods to build a connection with another person. Imagine you're engaged to someone. Have you learned their innate or preferred ways to give affection or build acceptance in a relationship? Do these methods meet your own needs for feeling wanted and appreciated?

Before marriage, learn how the other person does love. Love is an action. How does this person live it out daily? Does he or she do it in a way to make you feel it in your chest, or does it leave you uninspired? Look, we ain't talking about the "Love-At-First-Sight" kinda love. Most do feel this way in the early stages of courtship. It is simply unrealistic and not sustainable.

HISTORY & HIDE-OUTS

Meet Norah. A few other words to describe her are as follows: Polished. Educated. Attractive. Always helpful. Sadly, Norah, a divorced mother of one, is engaged to David, who doesn't choose the most admirable words when speaking to her. Surely, this is not a good thing, but it gets worse!

David dismisses small agreements such as meeting for dinner or attending a well-planned family gathering. David tells Norah his schedule got him distracted or time got away from him. He's a busy man! Besides, Norah knew this about him. They've known each other since high school. He gets frustrated because Norah never seems to understand his reasoning.

Each and every time, he's got one! Norah feels stung in her heart. She doesn't feel valued. Had she known life with David would be this way, she'd rather have remained single! Norah continues to tell David it seems their marriage isn't a priority to him.

The last and final limit for Norah was David missing her mother's retirement party. She'd been planning it for weeks. Dried tears stained more than her face during the event. She forced a fake smile to keep up appearances. Her problems would not rain on this lovely moment to honor her mother. She told guests David had an emergency meeting for a very promising business deal, and his flight was delayed. Everyone nodded, offered congratulations for the "great opportunity." Everyone felt assured David would pull it off triumphantly!

Later in the evening, Norah felt humiliated when someone shared David's social media postings of himself shooting pool at a local grill. How dare he embarrass her this way? Infuriated, Norah vowed to cancel their wedding plans.

Life with David would be rough. His shortcomings are visible due to their impact with scheduling, no-shows for events and certainly Norah's mood, it was notable to many.

No one heard the way Norah swore at him and called him names privately. When working on an average household project, like cleaning the garage, Norah's language reduced David to child-like levels. David would stare at her while she gritted her teeth and spewed words of contempt at him.

Once, Norah threatened to call the police on him if he said or did anything to negate her vile words and accusations. He'd respond by going for long drives.

Over time, he became more and more distant. He heard the whispers about he and Norah. Friends, an uncle, and even an elder in the family spoke to him privately about his treatment towards Norah. The first time he described how he experienced Norah, his friend was in disbelief! Not sweet Norah! David vowed never to speak of it again. He decided it was safer to leave the relationship quickly, while mentally and financially intact, and to allow Norah to retain her prized possession, a false perception of who she really is. She'd threatened to dump him anyway but had yet to make it official.

David prepared himself to be the "Bad Guy" in the eyes of others. Somebody warped Norah's perception of herself. She couldn't see her role in the demise of her relationship. Publicly, her manners gleamed. Privately, her attitude rotted from its core! Norah kept this information confidential until she was behind closed doors!

Norah's inability to be amiable with her husband as she was with everyone else prevented her marriage from having fairness and love. Norah would rather divorce before admitting her role in the marriage destruction. This is how the lack of self-awareness kills a marriage.

Did Norah learn this behavior from someone? Has she become so accustomed to the "Cover-Your-Ass" concept from her high-pressured corporate job that she does it off the clock too? Does her family have a history of looking the other way and keeping up appearances to distract from the problems no one wants to address? For what reason is David unwilling to hold Norah accountable? For now, he avoids the situation and opts to split versus doing the hard work of relationship recovery.

All it takes is one lousy relationship lesson with a family member, friend, colleague, or Bae!

This is how the relationship rotation goes around and around like a wheel. How does your relationship wheel spin? Maybe your wheel taught you to spot trickery a mile away! Or, you learned how to detect true love when you feel it. Maybe you were taught to keep your guard up, making it difficult for someone to love you. Are you inclined to withdraw from a relationship versus offering grace and safe spaces for dialogue?

Let's look at the relationship from 400 feet above. If you're peering down, you see your relationship history and the habits connected to it. For example, you have traditions and special memories with loved ones. Does your family have annual cookouts? Do you meet on Sundays at the home of a relative? Maybe you get a big smile when you recall the annual Super Bowl tradition your family has? Do you traditionally celebrate your birthday for the entire birthday month with your friends? Did you pray a specific way at dinner time when growing up? When you arrive at work, are you the employee who spends 15 minutes getting coffee, uploading your computer, opening the must-have apps to get you through the day, and position your headphones just right? These are all traditions and patterns!

Some routines and habits, you need to rid yourself of. Others have made you better to the degree that continuing those patterns give you more euphoria in life. Your relationship history and patterns flow like a river to current day connections. You react and translate the actions or words of others based on retired memories.

For example, let's say you have an attraction to people committed to their dreams and passions so much you don't recognize he or she can't commit to you. You admire the passion and purposeful love this person gives to their business, their artwork, or their activism. You believe, "If Bae can love a project this way, then loving me will be easy!" However, the love never transitions from the business plan or the last town hall meeting to embracing loving on you. The person is committed to their dreams. Nothing else! You decided Bae would replace their favorite interest with you.

Let's say your father and mother spoke to one another a certain way. Your violated parent hid their butt-hurt behavior from you as a child, and you want to do the same. You've been married twice. A deal-breaker for you is debating, arguing, or even hashing out disputes in front of your child(ren). Your parents didn't do it, and neither do you!

While previously married, you hated when your Ex insisted on deliberating an issue in front of your child. It didn't matter what it was! You resented your Ex for being so inconsiderate in a delicate moment. Your Ex said you wanted to sugarcoat the world, to protect the children from life, and you weren't teaching the children to negotiate their way in the world. You could not change this person's dang mind. This matter became another nail in the divorce decree on the wall.

This isn't about who's right or wrong. You value not having serious discussions where children are, and that wasn't acknowledged in your marriage. You learned this from your parents, but your Ex didn't hold…didn't see, and to you, didn't care about this same position. Your Ex grew up in a home where parents didn't yell but handled what they needed to in front of the children.

How do you rid yourself of the role you play in choosing people like your Ex who don't share your values, selecting unavailable people, or those who trigger your weaknesses? How do you stop feeling comfortable around people who don't call you to good, based on the way you define it? When do you begin to block lousy behavior and mistreatment? How do you rewire the glaring images taught to you through relationship history?

Take responsibility for your part in the relationship! Choose folks aligning with you and your values. This does not always mean a person from your old neighborhood. This may not be the man you went to high school with or the lady you had a crush on since elementary school. Do you know what this person has lived, loved, and lost since the last time you saw them? This is what makes the core of a person. If you don't know how they've lived, loved, lost and the experiences shaping them, you can't say where their heart and head are.

Familiarity doesn't make a marriage!

Being told to assume accountability for selecting a suitable partner causes many folks to run for cover! If you are ready to be loved well, grab the reins and hold on. You can do this. If not, wait a while. Someone will show up willing to violate the things you hold dear. We promise! For those holding on to their end of the love rope, let's review the things you need to be inspired and to have passion in a relationship.

To move away from the dim and dull place of feeling "Bae-Ain't-Coming," evaluate, assess and be straightforward about ways to create your best love life as well as who and what you DO or DON'T have in place, RIGHT NOW, to make it happen!

What Skills, Spirituality, Family/Friend Networks, Character Traits, Finances, or Education Do You Need to Establish the Marriage You Desire?

1. _____
2. _____
3. _____
4. _____
5. _____

For those willing to dig deep and lay their flaws out for a private viewing, let's gather around and see what you're working with!

To select the best relationship for you, you'll need authenticity and personal honesty with yourself. The easiest person to play games with is YOU!

Instinctively, you want to believe the untruths you tell yourself about you! Now, imagine being in a judgment-free zone and going from fearful and confused to purpose and assurance.

So, if you've been two-timing, have a history of being disingenuous, have/had an addiction, struggle with sexual deviation of any kind, carry stories of being the perpetrator of domestic violence, or you acted a fool and didn't display your best self in the relationship, please admit it right here. We're not asking you to agree with everything anyone has said about you, but if it has been spoken, alleged, filed in the courts, reported to the police, or documented, you know. You know who you are and the exact incidents causing folks to leave you alone, to divorce you, to file a police report, to unfriend you on social media, or to block you. You may agree you have the burden to bear in the demise of your previously flat-lined relationships.

What causes you to show up this way, recurrently, in relationships? You've gotten the same complaints with every partner. If not every partner, those who know you give the same complaint frequently. Your default response has always been to DENY or to diminish the other person's experience. Over time, this response has lost its luster. Your shea butter shine is gone!

Time and time again, folks telling you how you accept no blame, or you like disappointing others feels awful to hear. This is not who you are as a person! Yet, you remain in these brazen, hurtful, suppressing, overwhelming, and draining relationships or recreate them in serial succession and hurt someone you love and you. This isn't commitment! It's a foolish attachment. It equates to an unhealthy habit you've decided works for you despite the results on others and yourself. You've become attached to the complex emotions and thoughts from bad relationships. It's an addiction!

These instances cause pain, depression, bitterness for you, and the person you love. But you choose the same like-minded people to love, to prevent being held accountable for growth, but there's nothing off-key about you in your mind. You can't hit the LOVE BUTTON for the rest of your life if you continue to make these choices. You deserve to have better, even if it means growing internally. Avoid the restricted vision of Norah! You can do this!

List Unfiltered Truths About Yourself You Don't Like to Own!

★ _____

★ _____

★ _____

★ _____

★ _____

COMMITMENT CLOSET

Let's review commitment, relationship affirmations, and the conditions. In your eyes and future vision, how does a steadfast marriage walk and talk daily? You can easily list what commitment does not do. Loyalty does not cuss people out regularly or for no reason. Commitment doesn't tell folks, "I don't need you…Get out of my house!" Commitment doesn't talk to old lovers, knowing this upsets your partner. Commitment doesn't deny wrongdoings and never apologizing because you don't believe anything is off base despite what your partner says.

Insert your list of pain, anger, prior bad marriages and Exes, and the ways your idea of commitment did not show up in your past relationships. If you are bold enough, include your noncommittal actions, too!

Acts of Abandonment, Neglect, or Lack of Commitment in My Prior or Existing Relationships

1. _____
2. _____
3. _____
4. _____
5. _____

Ways I Failed to Be Committed, Based on Opinions & Feedback of Others

(You don't have to agree. You know what folks complained about to you or expressed disappointment about. Own it. Admitting what was said doesn't mean you approve of what was said.)

1. _____
2. _____
3. _____
4. _____
5. _____

For all the times you got that sound, flying-high committed love, describe what it looked or felt like here. What did the other person do for you that felt remarkable and said, "I got you!" to you? Identify actions or incidents that demonstrated loyalty to you.

Criteria and Actions that Look Like Commitment & Loyalty to Me

1. _____

2. _____

3. _____

4. _____

5. _____

CHOOSING TO BE COMMITED OR CHOOSY COMMITMENT

Stephen, a 42-year-old husband, father, and successful writer, has written many 'How-To' books on financial management. He and his family enjoy his success. His wife of 12 years, Linda, takes care of the three children. Stephen does it all! Linda's friends envy the way he helps at home, dotes on her, and cares for his mother. He can do so because of the flexibility in his schedule. He makes sure his family benefits from his time. Stephen pays a large portion of his elderly mother's bills so she can be comfortable in her old age. He is the man!

Often, this couple is doing well. The marriage has a few bones of contention, but what couple doesn't? Sometimes the children act up, but nothing major. Linda feels overwhelmed, but as a family, the couple manages and feels happy. Their sex life is active, and date night is twice a month.

Stephen has two children from prior relationships in his mid-twenties from two separate women. He has no contact with these children and never has. Linda knows about his other children. He told her during their courtship to "be transparent." She's never encouraged him to be a father. Yet, by all appearances, Stephen appears to be a committed father and husband with Linda.

Stephen has made a deliberate choice about what and to whom he will be attached in his life. He chooses to be elusive to the children from the previous relationships as he lovingly cares for the three children from his marriage. Does this behavior exemplify the type of commitment you want? Many admire and desire the lifestyle of Linda as a kept woman. How secure is she? Stephen can choose to treat her as he did his flesh and blood at any time. She is not exempt. She can be divorced. He can't divorce his kids, but yet and still, he walked away from fatherhood.

This is choosy commitment. Stephen attached himself to the idealized version of the life he seeks versus being committed to the choices he made, including taking responsibility for the children he fathered! The children from the previous relationships remain innocent but don't fit into the mold, model, and existing plan he has for himself. Consequently, his children remain hidden and lack the love and presence of their father. Linda is safe if she doesn't remind Stephen of his shortcomings or challenge him on his lifelong vacation from parenting. Stephen doesn't even seek to be "Uncle

Daddy," the father providing occasional child support and visits on holidays packed with loads of expensive fun a single mother can't afford.

You've met a man like Stephen. You see him at work. You see him at places of worship. He's admired. Looking at his relationship history, you wouldn't choose a man like him to father your child. Parenting isn't temporary. It's a lifelong commitment, but not to the Stephens of the world!

Ok, we all get an opportunity to waver or to make mistakes, but choices such as choosing not to parent should not occur! Do you want to begin a new life with a man like Stephen, who knowingly decides to ignore the lives of the children he fathered? Before you choose to be committed to someone, look at their whole relationship history. It isn't a final tally, but it is a great predictor for future behavior and values.

Now, let's go back and define commitment in action on its most basic terms and in daily life for you. If COMMITMENT had legs, arms, and mouth, how would it behave? Is "Uncle Daddy" behavior on your list of Commitment Conditions? Probably not. If a person does not exhibit your values for commitment in totality, leave them alone.

Linda lives a good life if she doesn't urge Stephen to be the man he says he is. For their marriage to remain happy go lucky, Linda must go on pause.

Regarding commitment, can you be so committed to keeping your relationship that you abandon your commitment values? Linda did. Don't be like Linda. Linda would tell you not to be like Linda.

Relationships have two types of principles, foundational and negotiable. Foundational values are unwavering. These include matters such as culture, religion, commitment, being debt-free, or structured eating habits. Other matters are up for discussion and negotiation.

What are your non-negotiables? Please refrain from using a faith-based list. If God has already stated the behavior as sinful, you don't need to reiterate it. Thus, adding a drug-free lifestyle or no infidelity isn't necessary. These are generally understood to be true. Identify your preferences for "What You Not Gon' Do!"

My Honorable List of Non-Negotiables in Marriage

- _____

- _____

- _____

- _____

- _____

CHAPTER TWO

THE FLAWS OF ATTRACTION

Misery loves company.

Happy people are magnetic.

Birds of a feather flock together. You attract who you are.

Some of you take these to mean you're destined for homelessness because the man or woman living on the street corner shoots their shot with you regularly. Not so! You'll be physically appealing to many despite any differences in opinion or lifestyle. But the individuals who continuously feel drawn to your personality do so for a reason.

Patterns exist in your choices due to stenciled behaviors traced repeatedly or from your own unmet needs. Have you ever been thirsty you can't stop drinking? Nothing will quench your thirst! And you look thirsty as you continue to go from one person to the next, trying to have your needs met while drinking from the same broken faucet! You don't even realize you're doing it!

Amina, a divorcee, is a lovely girl and has always been told so. She is 32 years old and mothers 2 of the sweetest children! She works as a dental hygienist and volunteers to provide dental care to the poor. Amina caught the eye of a dentist she met at a volunteer event, and he caught hers!

Jamaal, the single dentist with one child living with his mother, looks good like God took His time creating this man. Jamaal acts respectfully and wears pricey handmade Italian shoes. He delivers lunch to her job and her co-workers, occasionally, as a surprise. He sends the sweetest texts, including the official "We-Almost-Cuffed" texts in the morning and at night.

He takes her on dates to events and places she has never been before since they met 3 months ago. Amina likes what life with Jamaal looks like! Yes, she feels euphoria with him, and he echoes the sentiment. She has found a real man to give ease in her life. Amina has been very honest with him about her prior marriage. She told him she had no idea of what being a wife and mother would be like. When she married, it took her a few years to figure it all out. She was not raised by her mother but grandparents. Jamaal cannot imagine this being her reality because he watches the way she loves her children. She looks like she should birth his babies! He understands the difficulties of marriage and how hard it is when marriages don't work out. He empathizes with her. To him, she presents as an amazing mother and woman. He tells her often.

Amina feels annoyed when he doesn't answer calls in the evening or when Jamaal becomes distant on weekends with no contact. She blames herself because of her limited access to childcare. She and Jamaal can't go out on dates without the kids at times. She doesn't feel Jamaal should have to stay in the house because she can't go out. She doesn't ask questions regarding his whereabouts because he is a grown man. She wants to respect his space. Jamaal doesn't respond to her texts or calls. When she had a flat tire on a rainy day, he didn't respond for hours. However, when he did, he offered to send a friend to help her. Amina had a new tire already. She smiled and felt happy he offered help. To her, this meant he cared.

When she and Jamaal are in their zone, they text for hours and swap funny memes on social media! She accepts the parts of himself he is willing to share with her. She reciprocates by keeping things calm. She doesn't want to argue or start trouble. Amina wants to be easy breezy to entice Jamaal to marry her. No man wants a loud woman and with two kids. She needs to show whatever talents she can summon! Besides, Jamaal's absence isn't profound because he hasn't said their relationship is serious. Amina remains in an eye-on-the-prize position and gives no other man her time and attention, except Jamaal. She feels it would be too confusing.

Jamaal loves women, pays regular child support, and sees his son on his assigned days. YOLO! And Jamaal is getting all of his best life IN! He likes Amina, too, but Jamaal prefers Jamaal! She doesn't hold him accountable, nor does she ask for much. She fulfills his need for fun and companionship. Who doesn't want to be considered "Fun Girl"?

Amina is an adult woman with dreams, goals, and children. She needs an accountable man in her life with strength and leadership. Yet, she continues to choose men who aren't. She feels she has a diminished status as a divorced mother, so she asks for little, so men will not run from her. Jamaal looks like the best man for her, so she will wait to see what he decides to do. Jamaal can provide, makes her feel good about herself, and he is so much fun! Besides, what if no other man shows up as good as he is? From all the other ladies swarming around him, he chose her!

Amina sees herself in a weakened status and tries to hide her low self-worth. Her pretty face shields a broken heart. Thus, she is often placed in the role of the "good time girl" and not the position of a potential wife. She does not make demands or relationship requests. Thus, she opens herself up to being available to whatever a man gives her because she needs to feel wanted by someone. Because Jamaal dislikes obligations, other than the one he selects, he is more than willing to be the man to give her whatever it is she does not ask for freely! Furthermore, Amina's adoration for Jamal is unequal to his. Her heart has exceeded his threshold for her! Amina's actions are unreasonable because she's told herself this experience is bliss. And it is, but this thrill isn't permanent. Love wears out like clothing. Love will fit you well. Then, it becomes worn. Love requires renewal, proper care and treatment. Amina anticipates feeling this way about Bae forever. She'll be disappointed. This doesn't occur in the best of marriages. Amina has never witnessed or experienced the Care Instructions for marriage. When will she need to use a warm love temperature? What does a gentle marriage cycle look like and when to use it? Because of Amina's warped view of enamored love versus being deliberate about showing love, she's unable to be rational within her head and heart

What Are Your Care Instructions for Marriage? What Do You Require When Your Feelings Are Stained with Anger, Happiness?
or Feelings of Betrayal?

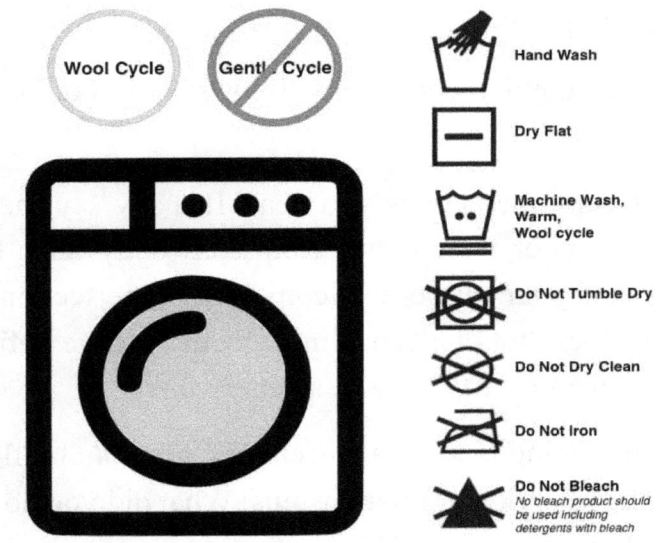

1. _____

2. _____

3. _____

When you are weak or have unresolved relationship issues, you'll find someone to help you continue to be limited. Their role won't be to assist in the repair or to take care of your heart, but to make wounds persist because you don't require or request a remedy or pain management. You attract how you feel about you, the good and bad. Fears and doubts hide in your secret crevices you don't want to admit to do exist. However, on the other hand, if you continue hearing you are not reliable, you may not be. If you continue to hear you have co-dependent relationships, maybe you do. If you're told you have a big ego, you may give off this vibe. If you are engaged to a person who is committed to everything, except you, "Houston, we have a problem!"

Listen to the things people tell you about you. Seek to correct yourself.

Don't deny the actions you hear. If many say the same thing about you and/or your relationships, err'body ain't lying! Now, sure, you and your partner will come with imperfections and faults! Everyone does, but don't maximize them or leave deficits to grow because you aren't trying to be a better you.

The next thing is to do a sincere inventory and reflection about self. Look at your other relationships. What did you do right? What did you do too much of? What role did you play in the demise of the relationship? What could you have done better? When could you have been quiet or said something better?

Amina is downplaying herself by accepting Jamaal's behavior. She can't change him, but she can choose to walk away. She chooses not to do so. Jamaal isn't willing to give her what she wants and deserves. He has no room to love her because he is in love with himself right now! She should take a cue from him and love herself, too! Being involved with him lowers her self-esteem more. Ok...yes, he tells her she is a good woman. He spends time with her, but he does not want to be in a relationship with her. He wants to date only, and per his schedule and preferences.

Jamaal will be a great guy for someone who seeks to date only and has no desire for a long-term relationship. Amina invites men into her life who help her to think less of herself. She will need to change her attitude, self-reflect, make changes to lure a different type of man, and treat herself better. The laws of attraction state we do things to draw and to appeal to people and events in our lives. Get this wrong, and you get wronged!

List Positive Traits About Yourself You Hear from Others

1. _____

2. _____

3. _____

4. _____

5. _____

6. _____

List the Fears You Don't Want Others to Know

1. _____

2. _____

3. _____

4. _____

5. _____

6. _____

Love, fear and loneliness, "The Cousins", have incredible powers that are not always used for good. "The Cousins" will have you driving across country, wearing a bathrobe and pajamas, in the middle of the night because you're afraid you've lost Bae for good. Or you saw a social media post and you need clarity about something that isn't your business, nor did it have anything to do with you! Any one of "The Cousins" will make you lose your mind and yourself! Love, fear and loneliness will tell you, "You're grown. Have sex with strangers if you want to. You deserve to feel good. Right now!" Love, fear, and loneliness say things to you, such as, "It's been 5 years. You're still alone. No one wants you."

Each one will lie to you, together or separately, cause overthinking, and urge you to make poor choices to make one or all of them go away. Be courageous. You can handle "The Cousins" and not allow "The Cousins" to control you. Together, their tactics are lethal to your head and heart.

Love will be an amazing, but temporary feeling of delight. This love doesn't have a foundation, is rooted in the potential or vision of the person you've elected to like, but not the reality of them.

Fear leads you to doubt your intuition. What if you're wrong about the suggestions your gut is giving you to walk away? If you don't marry this person, it could be your final option for the rest of your life? Those of you who've been divorced for many years tell yourself this negative thinking. These actions are self-defeating and reaffirm your unproven fears more. Fear will tell you it's too late to back out of planned nuptials. What would folks say about you? The unwarranted misgivings you implant mentally speak to you in the form of judgment. You're willing to risk getting a divorce versus be subjected to shady public opinion. In any case, none of your fears have actualized anywhere with the exception of your mind.

Loneliness has no decorum or scruples. Lack of companionship feels isolating and urges you to lock down on negative self-talk. To give an instance, this Cousin will tell you, "Call (insert name here). It's better than being here by yourself." You have no interest in this person, but you'll dial the number. Or you consume drugs or alcohol to silence the zealous throbbing of the heart. Others have used casual sex to close the need for closeness and being wanted. When the subsequent realness of being used for your body only sets in, more disappointment develops. The Cousins create outlandish damage to a life.

When you decide you lack the resolve to go home or to decline a date when you know you are sex-deprived and want to be held, everything within you will lead you to spaces of low self-worth. You lie in bed, praying for God to remove the angst of being alone or unmarried.

Don't forget one crucial detail. The path to marriage includes not being married. This is a part of your journey! God hears you. Because He does, your unmarried lifestyle, when done in a way pleasing to Him, has been mapped out to lead to Bae! This phase of life ain't holding you back. It moves you forward to the very thing you desire.

Mia's mother, Faith, was "The Cool Mom." Mia's friends confided in Faith, hung out at their house on the weekends. Mia idolized her mother for the ways she'd overcome so many uphill battles with money and men. Their relationship was close but had healthy mother-daughter boundaries.

Mia's stepfather, Joe, fits well with Faith. The two married while Mia was in high school. Their finances improved a notch with the union, but not much. Mia felt happy with Faith being in love. She'd never seen such a relationship previously.

Mia had seen other men beat Faith. Faith had three marriages end in divorce. Each marriage included violent acts with objects flying, broken bones, cigarette burns requiring skin grafts, and many nights of temporarily fleeing to safety. Only to return within a few days. This marriage didn't have any of those appearances.

Mia had her guard up and hated Joe for the first two years. Her anger showed up because she was ready to be certifiably livid with him if he ever touched her mother. He hadn't, but in the event he did, Mia and her anger had a well-charged battery of rage waiting.

Joe, on the other hand, found Mia to be unsettling, quick-tempered, and insulting with her sarcastic comments. Mia butted in their conversations, joked inappropriately with Joe, and spoke to her mother with a nasty tone as she pleased. Faith blew it off as normal

"Girl World." Joe was glad she was a girl because he wanted to turn her world in reverse with discipline and "good home training." He tried to have patience as he noticed Mia did this with everyone. It didn't happen daily, but the outcomes were the same for those who interacted with her regularly.

Conversations often included statements such as…

"Mia, you should think before you speak."

"Wow…I can't believe you'd take offense to something unintended for you."

"Mia, you crossed the line flirting with my fiancé."

"Wait! I know how you are. Before you say anything, listen."
"Mia, you're so strong. These men aren't ready for you."

"Don't yell at me for no reason at all! What's wrong with you?"

Mia's disposition was ugly. However, she had a bad case of "Pretty Girl Problems." Because of her physical attractiveness, many would look the other way, time after time. Her looks would get her a pass. Her beauty also got the attention of men. However, within a few weeks, after speaking with her, a man would stop calling. Mia recognized the pattern of the man being "way too sensitive about a little joke" or trying to "…make me into someone I'm not.." before he stopped calling. If this is what it took to get married, she'd gladly remain single!

Mia idolized her mother's strength to leave abusive relationships. Unknowingly, she also unconsciously admired the destructive brute force of the men her mother tried to love. Mia never wanted to be overpowered by anyone. For her, the way to prevent being controlled and repressed by anyone was to have a rigid emotional shell. She appreciated the tactics others used to avoid her and to stave off her anger. She felt respected.

Mia has no idea being exposed to the trauma of domestic violence has given her a hardened core-shell. Mia's personality echoes her mother's abusers in her futile efforts to ward off bullies or rough treatment. However, she gives the same behavior she doesn't want. Mia tells others her mother's story of survival. She is a committed advocate for not accepting poor treatment from others. She fails to tell the narrative of what she learned from her mother's prior cruel husbands. This is the true story Mia doesn't read about herself.

To tell this version would require Mia to narrate the story of the frightened, tearful little girl, hiding in the linen closet, watching in horror as her mother's face struck the floor violently, leaving behind more and more blood each time. Mia doesn't want anyone to know Faith's second husband would take her for ice cream after beating her mother. Mia feels dreadfully guilty for looking forward to those trips after each drag-out fight. Ice cream has been her comfort food for years. No one knows the real reason for it.

Mia is afraid the story of Faith's endurance will lose its shine. Mia feels terrified a man will mistreat her. She feels sad because she's lonely and doesn't know what to do.

What stories do you tell yourself about your life because you want to believe them in the order you've convinced yourself? What beliefs have you held on to that do not serve you well? How does this impairs your ability to connect with another human being on an intimate level? In what ways has it kept you from being authentic with yourself?

You and Mia need to be honest with yourselves. You can present well and look pretty for a potential mate. The saying goes, "Pretty is as pretty does." The unhealed parts of you will come forward and speak for you, and to you, in multiple languages, such as heartache, social isolation, poor money management, multiple divorces, poor physical health, mistrust, and feelings of abandonment.

Your ability to bond with another person will be a dead end until you tell the truth about how pain impacted you and what you'll do about it now. If you couple with someone else in this unhealed state, you'll attract someone who'll love the unwell and emotionally diseased parts of you. If you elect to transform yourself, in the marriage, this person will resist this new version of you. It isn't the person you introduced them to, nor is it the part of you they fell in love with. Heal first.

Healing How-To-Help List the experiences, events, feelings, or sensations you internally tussle to avoid, keep secret, or never want to discuss.

What thoughts or feelings get you stuck or really cause you to feel down?

Tell the story/stories in your life you don't want to believe is/are true or happened to you.

What wrong beliefs or unhelpful patterns are you willing to release and tell the truth about to move forward?

CHAPTER THREE

FEAR FACTOR

Folks react to many things, knowingly and unknowingly. Fear evokes many emotions and instincts. Fear of abandonment causes you to push people away when you want them oh so close! Fear tells us we will be alone for the remainder of our lives. Fear says we will never have children. Fear, and our Ex, whispers, "No one will ever want you!" Fear urges you to remain silent, so you don't talk your way out of a relationship. Fear makes you accept mistreatment and disrespect because no one else is showing interest in you.

Fear of being unable to protect yourself as an adult because you weren't as a child can make you distrust others. Fear of guilt from past mistakes causes you to choose people who don't meet your basic standards. Fear causes you to disregard the feedback of friends and family. Fear keeps you in relationships you don't want to be in. Fear will make you go against your values. Fear of the pain witnessed by a parent will put your feet to the fire to make sure the same never happens to you. Using fears as a guide for a partner will put us at risk of what we don't have sense enough to fear, but it can also be debilitating.

MOMMA SAID KNOCK YOU OUT

Layla put the knife down on the kitchen counter. She has no plans to cut her husband, Ali, and she surely isn't about to hurt herself. She's not sure how the knife got there. She doesn't remember picking it up, but she knows clearly the fear and blood-shot rage causing her to pick it up. Ali slammed his dirty five-finger hand on the kitchen table she cleaned while talking to her. He invaded her physical space. He sounded like her mother's husband. Not her father, but her mother's husband. The man had never been a father in Layla's eyes.

Layla identifies her father as her mother's physical and emotional jail. Her mother's marriage imprisoned her and sentenced her to a lifetime of living with emotional trash. Layla vowed she'd be free of control, pain, and abuse in her marriage. Ali had always been a patient and caring man, but if he thought for half a second of a New York minute he'd be like her father, Layla knows no one would be safe. Consequently, Ali stood in the kitchen at grave risk of whatever Layla decides to do. The risk factors include a knife resting calmly on the granite top counter.

Ali feels stunned. He wants to talk to his wife, but she looks like a stranger to him. He can't find words. Ali tells himself he will have dominion in his own house. Getting stabbed at home was not on the agenda! What is wrong with this woman? He considers a gentle campaign for peace and to take a breather before discussing this fully. He looks at her in the kitchen and immediately knows it isn't the time for delays.

Layla paced from the kitchen to the guest room. How did she get here? She thought of her mother. Her mother would sit quietly in these solemn and volatile moments. Her mother would tell her not to make Ali angry. She must've done something wrong, and to not do it again. Her mother would say for her to apologize to Ali, to cook him a good meal, to ask God for forgiveness, and not to make Ali mad.

Layla said aloud, "I am not my mother."

Fear cannot exist in the presence of anxiety and security simultaneously. She no longer trusts the familiar comfort of Ali's arms. Fear led her to the knife and the sharp tension cutting into the division between her and her husband. Layla doesn't know how to start over in this situation. It hit, literally, suddenly. She only has a plan for protecting herself from the woes and force-fed agony of her mother but lacks a plan for resolving a problem with a good husband.

Ali barely hears her whispered affirmation as she spoke, but he understands her mental state has more to do with her than him. He taps on the wall gently to get her attention. He says, "Layla, I don't want your mother. I want you." Layla then understands she doesn't require her mother's terrors to chaperone her emotions because those anxieties could only monitor the scene but give no instruction for healing or reconciliation. When you allow your doubts, worries, and prior trauma to dictate solutions for you, the results are limited without the full richness of options. Sometimes, the creation of other possibilities rely solely upon you. Leave the unhealthy lessons you learned from childhood and family alone. The adverse messages and choices you heard were birthed from fear, from hearing half the story because you were in a child's position, or from the traumatic outcomes of family secrets. Fear feels unlimited and endless, but it is narrow and can be restricted, by you. Living in these distressful spaces will cause you to miss out on indefinite Bae moments. Accept the responsibility to transform yourself.

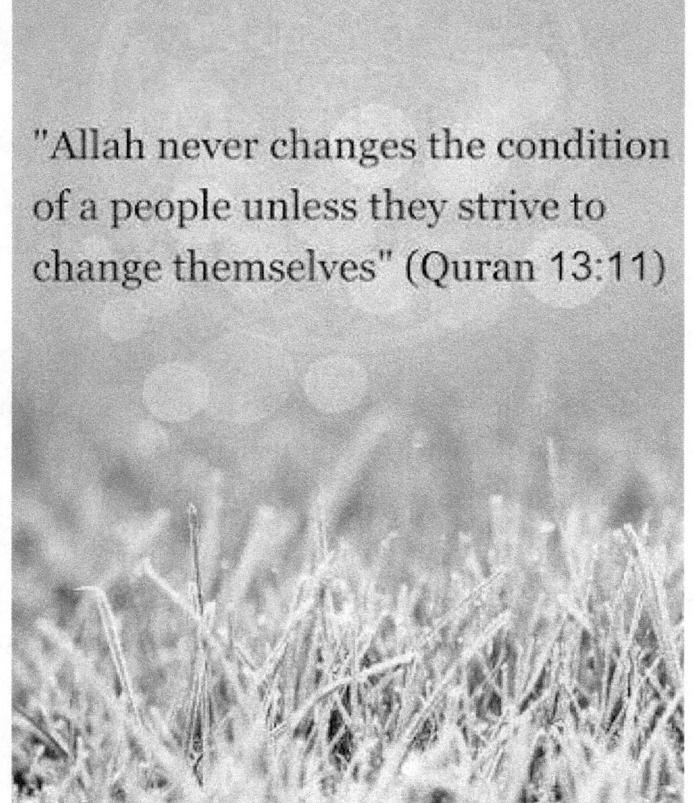

"Allah never changes the condition of a people unless they strive to change themselves" (Quran 13:11)

CHAPTER FOUR
GET YOUR "ISH" TOGETHER

Logan graduated from college, began working, and started his own consulting business on the side. Logan has friends, some are married, and others are not. Many of his friends envy his lifestyle and dissuade him from marriage. He considers himself a spiritual person but does not focus on enhancing his relationship with God. He prays and seeks to be a good person. For him, this is enough for now. He travels frequently and bought his first home this year. He feels content with his Bawse lifestyle.

Maryam has a life that mirrors Logan in many ways, with her work, intellect, physical appeal, and liberal beliefs. It makes him more attracted to her, and he can't wait to peer down into her pretty baby doll eyes. They discuss marriage. For some reason, getting married is hard to do. Sometimes, it is hard to talk after work due to scheduling. Maryam works overtime often. Logan enjoys FaceTime with her while he does research for his business. He can't FaceTime with her when she works late.

The couple exchange views about spending time with family during the holidays, but Logan has a project to work on. Maryam decides to go out of town with her sisters. Logan tells Maryam he didn't feel like he was a priority for her, which confused her. She feels perplexed and insulted. How could he say this, and she's been talking with him exclusively for six months? Does he have any idea how many men want to talk to her? When she shares the matter with family, she is advised to focus on herself. If Logan wants to be with her, he'll act like it. If not, Boy Bye! She takes a firm stance and lives her life.

Logan's friends suggest he moves on and meet on Saturday for an executive networking event. Maryam doesn't act like she wants him anyway. He's a good catch. She better act like she knows!

Meanwhile, she and Logan continue to talk less frequently. Then, the "I-Didn't-See-That-Coming" demise of Logan and Maryam erupts.

For Maryam, does Logan expect her to change her life around for him completely? He isn't her husband. Besides, she recently purchased a home and needed a roof replacement. Logan offered no money! She had to pay for it.

Logan thinks, "Does Maryam expect me to chase her?" Logan has a long list of thirsty and hydrated women desiring him. Maryam doesn't realize how lucky she was for him to look her way.

When you seek to marry, you transition your lifestyle to accommodate another person, including our attention. Being stingy with your time while expecting someone to invest or share time with you feels unfair. Also, never forget, when you marry, you pair up not only with Bae, but their entire family unit. Marriage is not the place for independence. Putting your priorities elsewhere makes you look selfish. How can it work out for you to be selfish while wanting selflessness from another person? Sounds confusing, doesn't it?

This imbalance also causes you to miss other important information you need for your level-up. You fail to see the authentic attraction a person has for you, what this person offers, and their short- and long-term benefit to your life. Does this person want to buy a home? Will driving a relative's car be sufficient versus buying a car? What is the lifestyle they're accustomed to? Is this person a victim of sexual abuse? Alcoholic parents? What will happen with their porn habit? Oh…you didn't know about the porn habit. You miss cues or clues for "real talk" scenarios reinforcing who chases who, who calls first or more, and being recognized for your fly!

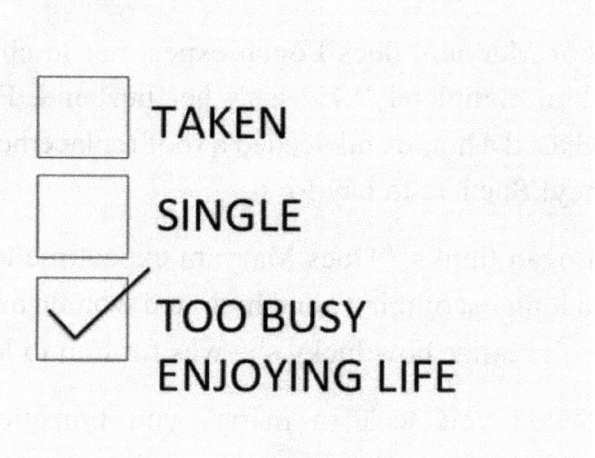

Establishing marriage begins before the marriage. It requires a mindset change, which includes the life you live and how you interact with others. Understandably, work schedules may not always be flexible, but Maryam and Logan missed valuable time when he decided to work when he wasn't at work, and she traveled with her sisters. This could have been an optimal moment to dig deeper into who the other person is and see the inner workings of family dynamics. Roots run deep!

Each person chose to do something else as if getting married were not a priority. This is what the single life will do to you! It will make courtship and the effort it requires appear to be cumbersome and inconvenient. If you prefer to be single, then be single. The single life is a crucial time for self-development and goal-setting. Don't skip it, but don't pull someone seeking a long-term relationship into your Single sideshow when you know it will be short-lived.

Also, be honest. Logan and Maryam fooled no one but themselves. Neither of them desires marriage, which is cool! Have the audacity to admit this when it is you! The judgement and opinions of others make folks reluctant to say so. Family and friends have their own timelines for marriage and family life for you. You are never required to live by these standards, particularly when you're not feelin' it!

Let's be ironclad honest and transparent. Family and friends function with limited information. The supporters of Logan and Maryam were TEAM LOGAN or TEAM MARYAM with nothing in-between to be friends of their marriage. Sometimes, our loved ones will find anything wrong with another person, and something can always be found! Sometimes, loved ones want you to remain single because of how your single lifestyle and freedoms benefit them.

Yes! We said it!

People who love you may not want the transition a spouse will bring to your life if it means you can't help them with their start-up business on the weekends, pick up their child from daycare, or be available for last-minute plans on Saturday night anything.

Next, look at their relationships. Are your friends and family members ideal candidates for giving advice? Some are. Some aren't. Take a moment to consider who you have in your corner. Take names!

Every now and then, those closest to us don't live out the best solutions and choices. They get to show up human also, but for now, this is about you and your relationship wealth!

If you're going to be authentic and hit a straight shooter, admit the angst of getting to know someone for lifelong commitment isn't always fun. As a matter of fact, it can feel painstakingly scary, crippling and cause anxiety while also heartwarming and fun. Healthy interests and productive distractions can balance out these topsy turvy feelings while putting in the work to find "Future Bae."

In reality, Logan will not be lonely anywhere he chooses to go.

Single, but not lonely! Imagine the fun Maryam will have with her sisters on her paid holiday time! The pics on Instagram will be lit!

Will this help them to know more about one another for marriage? Nahh.... Are Logan and Maryam supposed to sacrifice multiple opportunities like these to get to know one another? No. Logan and Maryam can engage with family while also making time with another a balanced priority. In a relationship, once you've decided to be committed, it's never all about you.

Securing your Love Thang requires accommodating another person with the intent to add mutual benefit to the lives of one another. Marriage is the level-up! Take your marriage to heaven. You can't get any higher than that!

Logan and Maryam said they desired one another. Their actions said, "Ahh...I'm not so sure!" They liked each other's company but weren't too excited about the steps needed to propel forward. They wanted to date and lacked the extended family and friend support to steer them in the right direction! We can become comfortable and feel safe in the lifestyle we create, even if we complain about an empty bed or the single life at times. Loneliness is real and causes us to make poor decisions. Ridding yourself of loneliness through a healthy relationship also requires the sacrifice of the single life. Yes, you see, to get married, you'll have to spend time unmarried! Where you are now gets you closer to the relationship you desire.

Marriage is not an island. It consists of two people of equal relevance. Logan and Maryam needed guidance and feedback during this process. Neither of them was getting good direction. Many adults don't accept the idea of getting guidance anyway. Many people feel and think, "I know what I want for marriage. How can someone tell me how to do it?"

No one is giving classes to make sure your marriage ends in divorce, but it happens at an astronomical rate! Married couples need pick-me-ups to stay connected! What will boost your moment, and will your spouse agree? Your thought process feels unproblematic to you, but that's to you! When tension and anger arise, no one's talking, and the baby is crying, what's the solution? Once. married, how do you fix this when your marriage lacks unbiased friends and family to give feedback? Logan and Maryam are engaged and have no one to rely upon for impartial input. With the exception of professional support, who could they rely upon for advisement after marriage.

Unmarried folks, the individuals lurking between being a couple and a married couple, need to transition into the married life, which means to wipe the residue of the single lifestyle. Oh, yes! The single life has stereotypical guidelines and expectations attached to it. Let's not pretend! And some of you do it, and more of you like doing it!

The issue with this is it means jumping directly from a courtship, if you even do that, into marriage, without taking the time to prepare your Single Self and the folks around you for your Marriage Moves! Your mother may need a minute to accept she cannot call on you as often as she did previously. Your ex-girlfriend may struggle with the idea that someone else has their head on your shoulder.

Folks pout because you have less time to visit as your wife or husband has family requiring time also. What about your friends? Friends stop inviting you to events as if marriage means you'll never be able to do anything. Ever. For-Never More. And it doesn't. Your natural circle will need to adjust to your married life. The way to do so is to begin the Unmarried phase, marriage preparation before tying the knot.

Having a robust and wise network of elders and advisors before marriage is a crucial safety net for you. You need real talk!

Married people who lived vicariously through their single life aren't valid relationship specialists! The mentality, effort, and sage networks needed to sustain a marital commitment begin before marriage. It may make you tired when you consider all of it! This aids in the success of relationships so much, it's worth it. Create a list of married couples to be friends of your marriage. Who will you contact first to inform them of this esteemed honor? Whoever you choose should be someone you know will be unbiased, have the eventual head nod of your Future Bae, not a family member, and will be respectful of your spouse.

Now, regarding family members, SMH…stay clear of those. While you may feel safe with disclosing information, your spouse may not. Also, you will forgive your spouse much faster than your relatives. If you and your Future Bae mutually agree to go to parent(s) for advice, we urge you to do so! However, have another list of standby candidates for this purpose as well as marriage mentorship. Ya'll, let's be honest. Many parents are not suitable marriage models. Your parents may have a 20-30-year marriage, but you know what it was like. Do you want to have their marriage? If not, learn how to implement other actions or you'll continue the patterns witnessed and learned.

Names of People to Become Friends of Your Marriage

1. _____

2. _____

3. _____

4. _____

5. _____

GOT MY MIND ON MY MONEY

Think of the last time you secured the bag! Did you save your dollars? Did you the freedom of a shopping spree.? There are folks who've decided money is to be spent. On the other hand, many consider this belief to be disrespectful to ways money can work for you. Do your financial principles with Future Bae align?

Nura has her apartment. Joshua resides with his brother. The two have been researching the market to buy a condo soon after their wedding. Surprisingly to Nura, Joshua has been cooperative and excited about the marriage ceremony. When he negotiated a great price for Nora to have the floral designs she wanted, she knew he was her man! His consideration for her was one of the most attractive traits about him. Her father happily agreed to give his daughter's hand in marriage as Joshua's future and character was optimistic. Finally, after many months, the condo search had been compiled to a list of 3 properties. Nura discussed the pending appraisals and her concerns about the unknown details of the buying process. Joshua calmed her concerns and confirmed a few details with the realtor.

Nura told Joshua, "We're going to need new furniture. I don't want the furniture from my place. You have to leave much of what you purchased with your brother. When can we go look?"

Joshua had arranged a deal with his brother to purchase key furnishings from him. He informed Nura. She frowned. She reminded him she knew nothing of this and repeated her dislike for the idea.

Joshua voiced his decision and said, "I'm not spending money on furniture when we have the basics. Furthermore, I won't reside in a home with fixtures and effects purchased by my wife. I don't care if it's your money. Besides, you're getting a wedding and a new condo within three months. Can't you be satisfied?"

Nura felt dismissed and slightly scolded by him. Joshua had been unselfish and diplomatic throughout their one-year courtship. Now, he acted self-absorbed. Nura wondered if Joshua believed he'd five and dime her throughout the marriage. Later, she presented the conversation to him again on the phone. This matter wasn't resolved.

Joshua relented, "You're right. I was dismissive. Buy whatever you prefer. I want you to make our house a home, but the key furniture pieces cannot cost over $200."

Nura asked, "Key furniture pieces? As in a couch or a love seat?"

Joshua replied, "Yes. So, you understand."

Nura commented, "Joshua, then everything we buy would be used or donated."

Joshua remarked, "I hope so! Wouldn't that be great? Preloved household items!"

Nura didn't want to be argumentative, but could he be serious? She and Joshua were amiable as long as they could quickly agree. When their financial values collided, it cost them their relationship. Nura had the insight to focus on the mindset of Joshua and not the event. For her, his convictions for budgeting did not match with her comfort standards. She wasn't willing to intertwine her life with Joshua knowing she would be expected to yield to his preferences, or her opinion would be ousted.

There are many common reasons for divorce. A false assumption is money is a top factor. According to clinical studies by The Gottman Institute (Gottman, 57-75), money isn't in the top four. The main marriage crashes are contempt, avoiding issues, defensiveness and criticism. Nura didn't know to say, "If I marry you, and you act like this, I will disrespect you and not like you." She could foresee herself feeling scornful towards Joshua over time. She wanted to be a financial partner in all areas and not be limited to when he decided he wanted her feedback.

Ensure your values are on the same plane. You can negotiate the destination, but each of you must agree to take the trip together and to travel by plane. See the pattern here? Having the same orientation about how to implement plans, including financial ones, will make or break a marriage. Many couples get stoked with the agreements made by each of them and never discuss how to accomplish a plan. Nura knew if she disagreed with Joshua, she'd experience a side of her that was unacceptable for her. She decided to cancel the engagement.

CHAPTER FIVE
ISSA NO FOR ME

We know the can of worms we're about to break open can't be yours, but maybe your friend did it, and now you can offer some wisdom. ((Insert a wink here)). We ain't saying this is you! It may be like some ish you did or a choice you made, but we ain't saying it's you!

> **Nope.**
> **No way.**
> **Not me.**

Please meet tall and handsome Brandon and the lovely Salina. Brandon is 35 years old, single, and he is FINE and smells good! All the time! God loves beauty because God took His time with Brandon!

Salina, a divorcee without children, is a health enthusiast and has a graduate degree in Economics. Salina has the prettiest smile, curves and keeps herself styled for an Instagram selfie daily! She works as a financial planner. She has several online profiles with dating sites and loves connecting with others via social media. She attends meetups to hang out with those having like-minded health interests.

Brandon and Salina connect virtually. They live several states away and converse through email and inbox for several weeks. He piques her interest! Naturally, Salina wants more information. He responds freely and does not avoid her questions. Salina likes this, and he makes her laugh. She inquires about his family. Brandon tells her he doesn't see them often as they live 5 hours away. This makes sense to her. You can't frequently visit with long distances.

He has lived in the area for 15 years. She wants to know what he does for fun and who his friends are. She hopes he likes tofu and homemade almond milk. He tells her he's an introvert, a private person, knows few people, and has never tried almond milk! Salina wants to introduce him to new things, and Brandon is willing. Not only do they have things in common, but Brandon doesn't belittle her interests or resist trying new things.

Salina emphasizes the relevance of God in her life on her profile. Of course, she asks about his faith. Brandon replies, "God and Me do our own thing. We're in tune. I don't get into organized religion. I'm a spiritual man." She accepts this because he didn't say he worships trees or has no belief at all! Salina has seen religious men and women act like jerks, so she feels cautious of religiosity.

Brandon likes her even more as few women react positively

when he tells how he feels about God. She tells him she has one child and discusses the struggles of being a single mother. She told him it would take time for her to loosen up regarding her Baby Girl to protect the two of them. Salina wants to keep the "crazies" from having too much information about her life until she builds trust. Brandon understands completely. He said he wishes his children's mother had the same mindset.

Brandon talks about his children lovingly. He said, "Their mother keeps me away from them. I want to go to court and have my children under my roof." Salina feels empathetic towards him and offers understanding. She commends him for wanting to be a father.

Brandon and Salina have more red flags waving than a fleet of ships! Salina lies, and Brandon is secretive. He answered her questions but gave no information for anyone to make a safe and sensible decision about him. He appears to have no familial, spiritual, or social ties. He gave no background details regarding the relationship he has with his children or their mother. What happened to cause this rift? Salina accepted Brandon at face value with the belief that better will come later.

In truth, both are being dishonest and evasive. For Salina, she told him she has a daughter because she has learned many men in her age range have children and get concerned about her ability to birth a child at age 36. So, in her mind, and virtually, she became a mother! It prevents men from questioning her ability to conceive or assume something is wrong with her, which can be an issue. Brandon mentioned going to court for custody of his children. He has been for not paying child support, but he doesn't mention this.

Over time, the deception and lies will come to light. Salina doesn't have a child. How do you hide that? These two have no sincere intentions for another person. One of the most significant issues with this is, often, one party is the disingenuous one while the other person holds on to hope. A well-meaning person gets strung along and has time wasted with someone running a game.

RED FLAGS THAT AREN'T ALWAYS RED

Brandon's secrecy is subtle behavior often used to deflect and to turn attention away from undesirable traits.

Many use this tactic, specifically in online relationships, to prevent a person from contacting others he or she may know or be connected with. It doesn't sound like secrecy, but will Salina seek to contact the mother of his children if she knows of the friction between them? Probably not. Salina makes a clear boundary regarding her daughter and legitimized her reasons. Consequently, Brandon will hesitate to obtain details about Salina's nonexistent lil' princess daughter.

Some folks present as a loner or shy, as Brandon does. You easily accept what this person says, 'cause it feels normal. Others don't want anyone in their business. These folks feel "haters" run wild, or people are "messy." Brandon describes his personalized faith-based relationship as being based upon.... Hmmmm, not very much, but it is his! It's a cloak to deter her from the truth about his lifestyle.

A woman such as Salina hides pertinent details such as prior marriages, her relationship with her young or adult children, or her inability to maintain a job as she prefers to keep a husband. A Brandon or Salina-like persona may be the person who has lived in a community for years and has a well-connected family. He or she works, appears quiet, and no one sees them often. You don't peep them frequently due to their alternative "down-low" lifestyle or their select group of friends who don't travel in the natural circles you do. For example, this person may use drugs. Another trend has been a person has mental health symptoms. This person, along with family members, work diligently to hide untreated mental health symptoms from you so you can be the one to deal with it. They're tired!

Meanwhile, family continues to witness outbursts, another good cussin' out, broken furniture, abusive texts, aggression, depression, or drug-induced states. These well-meaning relatives have decided the perfect solution is a "good husband" or a "patient wife" such as yourself!

Someone seeking a mate with strong family ties would be a good candidate for this person and their family. The family connection exists, but it isn't healthy, supportive, and doesn't have the components needed to sustain a marriage. How would you know?

We would be remiss not to introduce the man many have already met. He is the one for you! He insists upon secrecy for the sake of privacy, to avoid haters, and to limit distractions. For him, it helps to focus on the two of you and not what others think about the two of you. Unbeknownst to you, he is "kickin' it" with you and several other "private" women.

As a matter of fact, he's invited two or more of you to the same event. Each of you is so committed to his requests for exclusive secrecy that no one knew you were sharing a man. He's brave and overly committed but never committed to anyone. A key method for missing this train wreck is a well-planned journey. Don't jump on the first train to arrive!

Take your time. Ask questions, and don't be afraid. Typically, you aren't scared of the question. You fear the answer! Listen to your gut! You don't have to get a response to every question you have. If it doesn't feel right, repeatedly, walk away!

Your Instinct Kicked In

You Ignored It

?

Recollect times you ignored your intuition. What happened?

1. _____

2. _____

3. _____

Too often, you've ended a relationship, and when looking back, you see how much you did not know. How hurt you were when you learned the truth. Trusting yourself may be hard for you to do, let alone another person.

You'll never know everything about someone! Key issues such as distance, not asking questions, dismissing information given, and ignoring elder advice makes it easier for you to remain oblivious! Not wanting to hear wise words is not an excuse for a wrong choice. Don't choose to show up raggedy! You have a duty to ensure you're informed. If not, someone can use it against you.

ONLINE RELATIONSHIPS

Online relationships bring about companionship, make the world feel much smaller and allow us to meet others with similar interests faster. Lonely? Click a link, and you can have free or paid entertainment for hours! Have you heard about the joys of Canadian men or Jamaican women? Problem is, you live in Oregon!

Social media or a website can bring you together with love at first click! You love the accent and dialect of your online partner. Everything is great until you try to arrange a visit. Suddenly, this person becomes distant and sounds like your college roommate from Boston! Do you prefer a relationship with a good cook? Go online and meet a great chef who sends you pictures of meals! You don't know these are screenshots from Pinterest! Catfishing takes on more than a false identity. You may know a person's "government name," true physical appearance, and be bamboozled! Background checks and financial records can be falsified.

Nothing beats the direct face-to-face interaction and getting to see someone move through a few natural life scenarios. You don't know how a person handles anger until you witness their frustration. When you marry quickly, you miss out on getting first-hands peeps into the whole person because you marry the representative introduced to you but get mad about the actual spouse who shows up later. Put yourself on pause. Patience is a good thing when you're looking for forever.

Catfishing is also someone promising a lifestyle they cannot give you. An illusion! It does no good to have a great Canadian boyfriend who can't get a passport to the USA due to child support issues. Catfishing behavior includes your Island girl who likes girls as much as you do. The man promising to marry you who knows he can't leave the state due to his court-ordered joint custody is catfishing. He knows you live in Texas, and he's in New Jersey when he clicked on you! He can't afford to travel to meet you or to send for you. He continues to ask for pics of you in the nude or a preview of a specific body part. He doesn't plan to marry you. He enjoys the on-screen bond created.

You, on the other hand, continue to hope and pray it "gets better" and continues. Perhaps your man is a bit different! He requests patience until he gets his tax refund next year, and it is May of the current year. You agree. You put your life in boxes and a garage sale to relocate! The plane lands in his city at 10 a.m. The two of you marry before 5 p.m. at the local magistrate. Meeting someone to marry them is never a good idea! The emotional instability of such a choice is astronomical. Have some stamina. Your heart, head, private parts, and bank account will be grateful! These stagnant relationships and marriages are one-sided and include loss and heartbreak.

You can't get the information you need online. Naturally, folks develop an emotional attachment in online relationships. It makes it harder to break away even after finding out information that yells, "Run for your love life!" The heart hangs on to hope because of the imaginary relationship created.

The good news is people meeting online can have successful relationships; therein lies the difference. When you meet someone through a virtual connection, you've got to take it out of the matrix and transfer it to reality. You meet online. You introduce yourself and get to experience life with a person, face-to-face. At some point, and the sooner the better, the two of you will need to meet, to become familiarized with family, friends, and children, to learn about finances, faith, and simple daily living. If you can't do this, leave this person alone.

CHAPTER SIX

"WHAT DO YOU BRING TO THE TABLE?"

You likely have a well-rehearsed and frequently repeated statement detailing all you offer to a person, especially someone willing to jack you up! You have a cliché response consisting of some fundamental behaviors, such as, "I'm strong…I can provide…I am the table…My father taught me how to take care of a family…I cook…I'm a God-fearing man…I'm offended you even asked me this…I'm educated…I'm supportive…I can buy the table."

Well, whoop-ti-daym-do!

Others become upset with the question, "What do you bring to the table?" and refuse to answer this. To many, the question is demeaning, disrespectful, and has no merit. Don't you ask a potential employer what they offer? Do you not ask a server questions about the menu? When you're prescribed medication, have you not had questions about the full effects of the medicine?

Yet, when someone inquires about your benefits, side effects, and weaknesses, you become offended. Don't you want to know what the other person has packed in their swag bag of love, or do you prefer to rattle off your list of requests without being inquisitive? We promise you this is problematic!

Repeating your list of preferences and asking questions regarding bad habits you've seen before won't safeguard you from the lions and tigers and bears you thought to be extinct or never met before. Foolery changes its stripes and will turn to solid colors or smell differently! As a matter of fact, you can get introduced to new levels of "No-Act-Right" you've never witnessed after previously believing you'd seen it all!

- Remain curious.
- Don't make assumptions because you think you know.
- Ask for clarity.

Don't bring your table out for anyone to sit down until some essential criteria have been met. Your table should not be for everyone! Others with the same stand-up traits and desirable attributes you describe for yourself have been married, divorced, and lived in bad relationships for years. How will you use the talents and gifts only you have to preserve a relationship? What is your talent, bonus, or special sweetener only you can do like you?

Know your values and own your abilities. This information holds the secret to the longevity of your future marriage, but if you can't answer the question, the response remains a secret to someone seeking to love you! Having a directed and bona fide response for this question alerts a fool you are serious and know your worth.

Describe, with no ambiguity, your core principles and values. For example, you may sincerely require a spouse to share with parenting. For you, the absence of this gives the side-eye with a long glare! Provide details for what "sharing with parenting" looks like for you. Never assume because a person agrees they have the same belief system you do.

These methods don't stop all foolery, but it's the beginning of a full-blown deterrent.

A few questions to get your creative mastery flowing to display your top-shelf qualities and give your best with more precision about your benefits are right here:

1. What is/are your natural-born talent(s)? Make a list.

2. What have you been complimented about the most? Complaints others have about your personality or habits?

3. With people of the opposite sex, describe the feedback and comments you've heard the most about your personality?

4. Without using vague terms such as loving…kind…God-fearing…hard-working…what action/gifts do you offer another person, and how would he or she recognize it? What would you be doing?

5. With people of the opposite sex, what has been one of the most saddening comments or statements said to you?

6. What did you learn about love from your childhood and adults?

7. What gets you excited? Angry? Feel loved?

8. Identify an opinion given about yourself you don't like or agree with.

9. How much time do you spend alone and for what reason?

10. What is it you want a man or woman to see or to know about you as a roadmap to getting along with you well?

11. The past hurts, pains, and guilt you've endured, what have you done with them? If you believe your concerns are resolved, how so?

This deciphers the code to triggers and superpowers within your premium love package. Also, you can identify incidents or people sparking feelings of sadness or irritation within you with the speed of light! Repairing these emotional and mental potholes is your duty, but first, know them by name!

AT THE HEAD OF THE TABLE

Malik works and attends graduate school full-time. He also loves Aisha full-time, who is a college student, too. Their courtship has been for one year now. Both families approve and adore the couple. They plan to marry this year. They haven't missed a beat! They've taken their time, sought religious counsel, and enrolled in professional premarital counseling. Yaaasss!

In premarital counseling...

Counselor: *"What do you want from the other person?"*

Aisha: *"Whatever he has to offer. I like Malik, and he's shown to be a sincere man."*

Malik: *"I expect a religious wife and someone supportive."*
Counselor: *"What do you bring to the relationship?"*

Aisha: I cook and clean. I can take care of the home while he works. I'm not a loud person who likes to argue. I don't like conflict.

Malik: I love those qualities about Aisha. For me, my father taught me how to take care of a family. There were 4 of us. We were always taken care of. My mother had everything. A man works.

Aisha's comment put her in danger of abuse or being subjected to anything, good or bad. If she is willing to accept "whatever," what happens if she doesn't like what is given? What does she do when Malik does something she likes and then stops? She left herself open to way too much! She gave no boundaries.

Malik's definition of a religious woman is broad. How does he want her to show support? What defines a religious woman to him, and is Aisha that type of woman? And what does too much religion look like? Aisha doesn't want a husband who listens to religious lectures all day. Malik wants a devoutly religious home, but he also wants to listen to R&B music. To Aisha, this doesn't show religious devotion. Her parents taught her secular music was sinful. What happens when Aisha's spirituality becomes stagnant or progresses to a level Malik hasn't reached or doesn't want in his home?

Malik hasn't presented himself as dishonest because they haven't had an issue blow up, causing him to feel threatened or to protect himself from being exposed. Malik hasn't felt the need to safeguard Aisha by lying to her because something he did would pain her. These scenarios simply haven't come up.

Aisha doesn't know Malik has a child on the way with a woman from a previous relationship. She didn't ask, so Malik is clear from not telling her. He didn't lie. He just didn't bring it up. Malik is hoping she won't carry the baby to full term anyway. The mother has been having many complications. For him, it's a "wait and see" game.

Aisha displays the modesty and demure traits of the righteous woman Malik prefers. She practices the same faith as he does. She also takes part in tribal witchcraft taught to her by her beloved Aunt. Aisha performed a spell to meet Malik. Malik does not like "spooks," and for him, this violates his faith. Malik has not discussed religious practice with Aisha. For what reason? They attend the same worship services. Pray with the same people and use the same good book.

Aisha nor Malik considers these complex issues. And while there isn't a cookie-cutter question to prevent the scenario, discussion is vital. Each of them holds defining information about self and their mindset, which may be deal-breakers for the other person. When you fail to ask questions, you limit what you learn about the person, their lifestyle, and their vantage point.

Many don't ask because the explanation or reply given may lock out a person's potential candidacy as a spouse. When an emotional attachment has developed, the courage to let go ain't easy to muster up. Folks don't want to know a disappointing truth! You seize onto the person in front of you with the mysterious assumption of making it work, even when you see evident and subtle signs indicating it may not.

On the other hand, folks don't know what to ask, the answers to look for, or dismiss vague or confusing responses. Premarital counseling will clear this up for you. Also, consider the sage wisdom or seasoned advice of a community of elders.

Trust your judgment and get input as well. You are grown and make it happen in many areas of life. You got this! Yet, there's an issue. You dismiss the demise of your prior involvements and give yourself credit for what you learned in those interactions. You did learn much. On the other hand, what essential smoking-gun info did you miss to gain genius mastery of preserving a future marriage? Until sincere reflection occurs, your same bad habits hide in the corners of a pending marriage.

Let's go back to Aisha's statement. Cooking and cleaning skills are not high-level predictors for a healthy marriage. Millions of folks have this capability. How does cooking show the gifts you have to protect a marriage? It doesn't! Having a kitchen skillset is great, but people will eat, married or not! Now, a cook master surely makes for good meals and full stomachs, but won't keep you married.

Name your talents, décor, contribution, offerings, and all you carry in your personal swag bag!

Don't wait for someone else to tell you what your love skill set is. Many wait for marriage to "know who they are" and then get mad with the meaning given to them. Know what you bring to the table before you get the invite!

Identify these actions. How would you, or another person, know when you have displayed the actions on your Gift List? What would this person see you do or say?

Create your Gift List. Identify the Talents and Gifts You Have to Sustain Marriage

1. _____
2. _____
3. _____
4. _____
5. _____

CHAPTER SEVEN

UNDOING BEING UNMARRIED

We're gonna hit the target head-on for this one. Describing who you are and your lifestyle as an unmarried person will not give anyone an idea of who you are as a spouse. Listening to someone describe their existence as an unmarried person won't give you an accurate account of who this person would be as a spouse.

Folks want to envision a love, financial, spiritual, family, parenting, and sexual relationship with you in marriage. Common interests such as listening to the same podcasts on your way home from work, participating in the same sports, watching the same Netflix shows will not make or break your marriage. Getting excited about similar personality likes or dislikes means nothing. Too many get entrapped in this funnel and translate it into connection. It is on a very surface level.

Next, if you've been married before, be honest about how you showed up in the marriage and the ways your former spouse said he or she experienced you. Not your interpretation of it, but the language you were frankly given. You don't have to believe it, but disclose it. If you've done work for change, great! Say so!

For the unmarried person who has never taken love leaps of this magnitude, someone has checked you before, given a compliment, or your family has given a comment or two about who they feel you are. Tell the truth about what was said to you and make personal revisions.

We deliberately chose the word, "unmarried." There's an impressionable difference between a person living the single life and an unmarried person. An unmarried person has done the prayer work, got their cash in order, thought about their credit, decided to step-parent or not to step-parent, made relocation decisions, has boundaries and can state them, know what they offer, and can tell the coordinating and supportive characteristics needed to support who they are and what they offer, or come up short on, in a marriage.

Folks living the single life don't seek marriage. If this person meets someone, "Cool." If not, "Cool." A single person wants to "get to know people" or "to focus on their career" or "to get stuff out of their system" or to have a sex buddy with no strings attached. None of these lifestyle choices include obligations to another person or marriage. A single person may not say cliché "I-Ain't-About-The-Love-Life" statements to you, but their lifestyle will reflect it.

Does this person try to meet you at the last minute regularly?

Has this person ever gotten ready for a night with friends or an event while talking to you on the phone and never extended an invite?

Does this person want only sex from you?

Have you never met their friends, family, or child(ren)?

Are all or most of their friends single and living a similar lifestyle?

Does this person not speak about a financial future with you at all?

Has this person ever made long-term plans with you and never made the short-term action to make it happen?

When seeking information about "What are we?" is this person vague or says, "I'm not ready...Let's see where it goes...Don't rush...I'm seeing other people...?"

Is this person living in a place unable to accommodate a lifestyle for two with no plans to move?

Has this person ghosted you for days or at all?

Does the midnight hour catch this person out and about during a workweek?

These are all cookie-cutter patterns of the single lifestyle. If this is where you are, distance yourself from the head and hearts of people seeking commitment. Know yourself and be honest about it. It's not fair to be raggedy with other people.

CHAPTER EIGHT
"TRICK OR TREAT"

Randall admires the long talks, laughter, and confidence Jasmine has with her mother. Randall believes Jasmine and his mother will get along well. He hasn't told Jasmine this, but in his mind, she'll be a good mother to his children one day, much like his own mother.

After marriage with Jasmine, Randall gives specific events and close observations. He notices Jasmine confides in her mother about their marriage, including their sex life. He feels uncomfortable in his mother-in-law's presence. The thought of her knowing his personal orgasm history is unthinkable! His mother-in-law shouldn't know his kama sutra winning combinations!

Jasmine spends nights with her mother, unplanned, leaving him alone on a Friday or Saturday night. Randall never imagined a married woman having sleepovers with her mother. Jasmine calls her mother for viewpoints about their arguments, significant decisions, or something he said. His mother-in-law begins to be short and distant with him. He doesn't understand initially as he and Jasmine make peace, her mother shows her disdain for him for weeks. She smirks at Randall and looks at him, shakes her head, and raises her hand only to say, "Lawd, help my daughter," then turn her back to Randall. The mother and daughter interactions are excessive for his liking. Randall thinks his wife betrays his privacy and her mother has too much influence in their marriage.

When Randall tells Jasmine his thoughts, she immediately threatens to leave him and calls him a "jealous bastard" for wanting her to choose her mother or him. Jasmine reminds him, "I never hid my love for my mother from you, and I won't now. We've always been this way…How dare you bring this to me?!"

Randall was speechless. Randall had full wide-eyed awareness of the frequency and depths of Jasmine's dependence on her mother. Before marriage, he interpreted their exchange as healthy and traditional. Randall gave no forethought to how this level of co-dependency would show up in married life.

YOU CAN'T JUDGE A BOOK BY THE COVER

Karima admires the organization and discipline of Mohammed. As a researcher, his daily reading rituals from various journals and newspapers consume 2-3 hours of his day. Early each morning, he begins reading newsletters and listening to his colleagues' lectures on the morning route to work.

On weekends and evenings, Mohammed attends meetings with his professor friends from local universities or goes to one of their lectures at a local museum. He's also on the Board of Directors for a non-profit to prevent gun violence. His commitment to social justice is a turn-on for Karima. Mohammed has principles and ethical guidelines for his life. Karima knows a man with this type of strong wit and decision-making style would be suitable for her. Mohammed gives his opinion on finances and investments. She likes the way he tries to protect her hard-earned money. She accepts his advice, although a few times, Mohammed had been wrong. Karima lost thousands of dollars using his financial secrets. It wasn't his fault. Karima knows investments can lead to losses.

When Mohammed travels to Boston for a week, he rarely contacts Karima. She understands his busy life and keeps herself entertained in his absence. She'd promised herself she'd put no pressure on herself or Mohammed. They'd only known each other for 13 months.

Within another six months, Karima feels impatient about Mohammed's intentions. When will he propose?

Meanwhile, Mohammed continues his existing relationship in full-view of Karima. Mohammed has a romantic rendezvous in full bloom. He loves his "Bae" and has no plans of leaving. Mohammed is married to his research. His books. His academic interests. Competing with his scholarly friends. His daily writings. His record-keeping. His flaxseed smoothie recipes from Pinterest. Mohammed commits to his leisure and professional pursuits. Karima can't compete.

When you see behavior, good or bad, give a CSI-look peek into how this would look with you. Ask questions. Present options and see what a person chooses. Consider how your opinions and upbringing equate to the views of this person. If you "feel some kinda way," leave this person alone. You feel this way for a reason. Intuition is real. Don't get married and find out the extent of the damage or what it means later. It'll be too costly!

Karima will be a lonely wife married to Mohammed. His advocacy and loyalty to justice and scholarship stimulate Karima. And Mohammed, too! He'll bring suffering and resentment to a wife unless he changes. For now, this is who he is. Karima needs to go now while it's cheap and will cost her head and heart no more coins or time.

Randall views this mother-daughter relationship from his own rose-colored lens. Jasmine and her mother's relationship is nothing like his mother and sister. He takes one look at their interactions and makes an assessment. Decides it's cozy and aborts the mission for more information. He resolves he knows all he needs and sees a good influence on his marriage from his future mother-in-law. He's wrong. The relationship he witnesses with Jasmine and her mother is unhealthy and has never transitioned into a balanced parent and adult child bond. Jasmine's mother continues to guide and inspire Jasmine's life as if she were a teenager. Jasmine accepted her mother's involvement as she lacked will power and certainty in herself.

Randall never complains. Jasmine feels Randall trusts her mother as much as she does. She hasn't learned revealing her husband's flaws, bedroom talents and habitual delays to her mother put Randall in a tragic position. Jasmine forgives Randall long before the folks who love her do. Randall isn't allowed to forget the acts of mercy extended to him either. Any understanding granted on his behalf has a footnote and reminder attached by Jasmine's mother.

Randall and Jasmine are in the same marriage having two different experiences. Each makes assumptions and guesses about the other person based on the individual perspectives brought to the marriage. To fight against the terminal disease of what you think you know, ask the other person. Even when a person agrees with your position, learn the reasons for it.

Don't make broad-based assumptions about what you see and the meaning behind it per your life experience. ASK! Their motivation and spirit for action may not be the same as yours. If you're content with someone agreeing with you, have at it. This pattern won't work well and doesn't contribute to longevity. At some point, your internal driving forces will conflict. Learn the rationale and incentives for hiding behind actions and choices prior to marriage. You'll learn much!

TO THINE OWN SELF BE TRUE

Alana and her sisters have known Omar for years. They've always believed him to be a bit weird, but no one could put their finger on anything. He hadn't said or done anything harmful to anyone. The vibe given off in his company caused an unspoken discomfort, but no one could accuse him of anything, so they didn't. Anyway, he could be hilarious and had been the opening act for local events as a comedian. Through the years, Omar got fine, muscles, a college education, employment and was known for his integrity and faith. Alana quickly noticed his smile and grey eyes when his beard grew full, curly, jet black and called for her to lay next to it at night…in her mind anyway. He's never spoken an inappropriate word to Alana. Omar looks like Future Bae!

Omar and Alana begin dating. Their families feel elated. Like many parents, their natural and unconscious fear is their son or daughter would marry a strange fool, with alien family members no one knows! This union would be familiar and the perfect way to blend two families in the community. Having grown up together reassured the engaged couple of long-term compatibility. Next, Omar didn't have to deal with the embarrassing childhood stories his mother loved to share! Alana had been present for many!

Two months before the wedding date, Omar sits in the family room of Alana's parents. He'd been welcomed many times before, and this moment was no different. Alana noticed the phone and left him to himself. She goes to the kitchen to prepare a favorite family dessert with her mother. The house smells delicious from the delicacies baking in the oven!

Alana's mother leaves the kitchen, returns, and nudges her daughter. She points toward Omar and smiles. She's glad to have him as a son-in-law soon. She and her husband wanted Alana, and her sisters, to marry spiritual and high-principled men. As parents, making sure their future husbands were college-educated or worked in specific fields wasn't a priority. A God-fearing man was the top-notch goal!

Alana shyly smirks and glances his way. She quickly turns back to her kitchen tasks. Until a shape on his phone screen catches her eye. She turns her body completely towards him and stands still.

Wait...

What?

Could it be?

NO!

Alana shakes her head in disbelief. Innocently and unaware, Omar is watching pornography in the home of his fiancé with her and his future mother-in-law only a few feet away. Alana begins talking to her mother to distract her. She prayed, On God, her mother wouldn't be mindful of his iPhone screen. She sweats, feels her stomach become nauseous and light dizziness. Nevertheless, she continues talking normally.

Alana knows she must present this issue to Omar. How? Would he lie to her? How long had he been doing this? Is he addicted to porn? What else does he do Alana didn't know about? She grabs her shoulders for comfort because all of this felt creepy. Straightaway, she recalled moments Omar fixated on his phone screen in isolation. Once, she thought his hands were in his pants while doing so but quickly dismissed the idea.

UGH! Could she marry him? How would she stop a whole wedding? Her parents spent money! She'd been told Omar was one of the last of good men. She was blessed to marry him. Her dress was handmade lace and was stunning!

If she pulled out of this wedding, what would she give for a reason? She couldn't say, "Omar watches porn." Who'd believe her? And is porn so bad? He's young, after all. She knew he wasn't a virgin, so of course, he'd be interested in sex. Alana was no longer intimate with him. She stopped having sex with him four months ago in the hopes their wedding night would have a fierce level of passion. Omar probably started watching porn when she stopped having sex with him. For her, this made sense. What if this was all her fault? Could she have driven Omar to this unthinkable sin? How could she turn this around for him?

Of course not! When the relationship we've created in our heads, believed to be a reality, and has the head nod of loved ones, doing the moonwalk on a green love light feels rough! However, this may be necessary. The courtship phase is the time to make active decisions about the pleasantries and the negative actions. Assuming responsibility for inappropriate choices, value violations, or simple foolery will lead you to relationship gaslighting, blame, and feeling defeated.

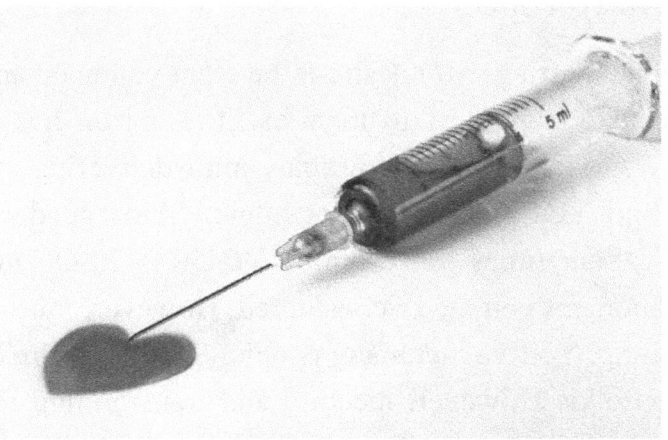

Alana's role is to be a wife, not "fix" Omar. Rather than face shame and judgment, Alana mistakenly theorized her ability to cure Omar. Even if she could, this isn't her role.

Taking on the role of "Critical Care Wife" puts her in the ongoing position to diagnose, to rehabilitate, and to restore Omar. Where is Omar's responsibility to himself in this matter? Alana let him off the hook! She sought methods to conceal the truth, avoid public embarrassment, not distress her family, and to set the well-lit stage for a marriage built on deceit and possible sexual deviation.

Alana's willingness to sacrifice her integrity and pending marital life creates a possible dynamic with unforeseen outcomes.

Pardoning someone for misunderstandings and natural human flaws is fair and admirable. Deliberate decisions leading to personal self-destruction has roots in flawed thinking. Protect yourself from this pattern. Notice behavior practices or lessons learned from others that have been normalized, but overall, are pretty unhealthy or toxic. Actions may be familiar, but this doesn't mean they're always beneficial.

Take-Away Time

For the marriage you desire to be what you need and want, you have to take steps now to manifest it. Amazon has an excellent delivery service, but for now, they ain't delivering spouses. You won't find YOUR PERSON at home. Marriage doesn't happen instantly. Sometimes, you can meet YOUR PERSON unexpectedly, or in a moment you never considered. However, meeting someone is one thing. You've met many people. Shoot! You're even tired of meeting folks. However, meeting and transitioning to "I want to know more about you…" ain't the same thing. This is how you reposition yourself.

Repositioning requires moving away from comfort zones and familiar places that don't serve you. We asked a young lady if she had considered her natural circle was not supportive of opening opportunities for the type of man she wanted to marry? This didn't mean her family and friends didn't want good for her or to marry. The real question is, "Within this group of people, is there a realistic possibility of meeting the type of man I seek?" She paused. She didn't like her answer. She knew she would not, with the relatives she had that were anti-men. She knew she would not, with the friends encouraging her to work more and socialize less. She knew she would not, with the business partners urging her to build her empire on her weekends. She knew she would not because her networks pulled her away from healthy personal relationships and more towards work and status. She then saw how the suggestions and networks, including friendly ones, were not about her building herself.

If her companions and confidants didn't have a marriage mindset and distracted her from her internal goals, how would she connect with anyone in such an impersonal environment? It ain't gonna happen.

Talking about marriage, resharing relationship posts and memes on social media, or binge-watching romance movies isn't going to draw YOUR PERSON to you. It ain't gonna happen. You have to create a premium relationship internally and let it move forward externally.

Have you ever thought, "Just as soon as (_____) happens, I'll meet the person for me, or I'll be ready for marriage"? There will always be something to work on. You can put effort into being your best self AND get a life partner or be married at the same time. Waiting for the perfect moment in life is an imperfect method. It ain't gonna happen.

There are a few truths we want you to put in your pocket.

1. You'll meet many great people at the wrong time. There will be a day on the calendar when your heart will come to a brief standstill. You'll meet someone who has strong

sexual energy with you. The vibe will be everything. But you won't be ready at the moment. Or you could be, but due to the situation with your mother's health, you're not prepared for marriage. Or you could be, but because your job is so unstable, you're not prepared for marriage. Or you could be, but you know you plan to relocate within 6 months, so you're not prepared for marriage. Don't dismiss the areas of your lifestyle that could be disruptive to a union. If it ain't working for what you're trying to do, how you're trying to feel, and how you want to love, toss it!

2. Ask yourself, "Does this fit into my plan to be the person I want to be and love the way I want to love?"

3. There are way too many "I" moments in this lifetime. In personal development, we've heard it's best to use "I" statements. It is, when communicating verbally. When you use "I" actions, it doesn't speak the same language. You look selfish.

4. Stop Blaming Expired Events and People. Your past did happen to you. Our past also happened to us. Do you see the pattern? Everyone has a past. You cannot continue to hold stale, uninspiring, and historical former times responsible for where you are today. Don't entrap yourself, mentally or emotionally, in those old moments. If you don't reposition yourself, you'll never digest the fulness of where you are today. Don't block you. Your family had traditions and habits. It doesn't have to be the way it was anymore. You've heard others speak to you a specific hurtful way often. It doesn't have to be the way it was anymore. Create

something new for yourself. If not, you will redesign the past with a new set of people.

5. List 4 moments of Self-Discovery gained from using this Premarital Guide.

6. What have you learned was a huge mistake in your prior relationships, and what will you do to safeguard yourself from doing this again?

There is nothing wrong with you. You'll make mistakes, and it is ok. You've been married multiple times. You've never seen a loving marriage. You grew up with abuse and love coexisting. You don't know how you want to be loved or how to tell someone to do it. You're so afraid of getting a divorce or selecting the wrong person. You haven't gotten married. There is much growth in knowing you, meeting you, and growing with you. Do this for you before introducing another person to the parts of you that you are yet to meet, including the ones you don't like so much.

As you grow, the lessons may be harder to hear and to see. One person who often struggles to learn a daym thing is a person who believes they've already learned it! Stay out of your own way with your assumptions. Unfriend your ego. Doing so leads to the gracious and loving path for securing your Bae for life.

REFERENCES

Gottman, J. M. (1993). A theory of marital dissolution and stability. *Journal of Family Psychology*, 7, 57 – 75.

Gottman, J. M. (1994). What Predicts Divorce? Hillsdale, NJ: Erlbaum.

Gottman, J. M., & Levenson, R. W. (2002). Two-factor model for predicting when a couple will divorce: Exploratory analyses using 14-year longitudinal data. *Family Process, 41*, 83–96.

www.ingramcontent.com/pod-product-compliance
Lightning Source LLC
Chambersburg PA
CBHW050657160426
43194CB00010B/1977